The Essential Air Fryer Cookbook for Beginners 2021

The Ultimate cookbook for beginners, eat fried food with easy and delicious recipes, lose weight fast and enjoy crispy meals

TASHA MANN

TABLE OF CONTENTS

Introduction

With technology giving birth to different and unique inventions every day to satisfy the hunger for innovation in society, the everyday kitchen's modernization is also seen. Among the many devices that have made life more comfortable with their usefulness and design, the Air Fryer is an excellent tool with many benefits.

An Air Fryer is a device that cooks food not by using oil but by heated air with no compromise on the dish's texture and flavor. Air Fryer is not only used for frying up food, but can also be used for many other tasks such as grilling, baking, roasting, and many more. It ensures the food is cooked evenly and thoroughly. Its design is such that it fits in a compact area and works via electricity. It has many different parts:

The frying basket: It is a stainless-steel basket in which the food is placed for cooking. It can be replaced by any other utensils, such as a pizza pan.

The timer: The timer is set accordingly; a red light indicates when the time has been finished.

The temperature controller: The temperature of the Air Fryer has a high range from 175 to 400F. Adjust the temp knob to achieve the desired temperature.

The air inlet/outlet: It is used to release the hot air and steam that arises during the cooking process from the device's back. It is, therefore, important that the device is always kept in a spacious area.

How to Start Cooking in An Air Fryer?

Firstly, the Air Fryer must be in a spacious place to allow heat to escape and prevent damage to its parts. It should be put on top of a heat resistance surface.

Secondly, pull out the frying basket gently from the machine. It is recommended to preheat the device for 5 minutes before using it. Simply set the desired temperature for 5 mins and then after the time is completed, pull out the basket.

Now place the food inside the container. Not more than 2/3 of the container should be filled. If required, the container can be greased with an oil spray to avoid sticking the food. If fatty foods are placed, add a little bit of water so that the container remains clean.

CHAPTER 1

Breakfast

1.   Creamy Bacon & Egg Wraps with Spicy Salsa

Preparation Time: 5 minutes

Cooking Time: 10 minutes

Servings: 3

Ingredients:

3 tortillas

2 previously scrambled eggs

3 slices bacon, cut into strips

3 tbsp salsa

3 tbsp cream cheese, divided

1 cup grated pepper Jack cheese

Directions:

Preheat the air fryer to 390 F. Spread one tbsp. of cream cheese onto each tortilla. Divide the eggs and bacon between the tortillas evenly. Top with salsa. Sprinkle some grated cheese over. Roll up the tortillas. Cook for 10 minutes.

Nutrition:

Calories 210.8

Fat 14.7g

Carbs 2.9g

Protein 16.8

2. Tomato, Basil & Mozzarella Breakfast

Preparation Time: 5 minutes

Cooking Time: 5 minutes

Servings: 1

Ingredients:

2 slices of bread

4 tomato slices

4 mozzarella slices

1 tbsp. olive oil

1 tbsp. chopped basil

salt and black pepper to taste

Directions:

Preheat the air fryer to 370 F. Place the bread slices in the air fryer and toast for 3 minutes. Arrange two tomato slices on each bread slice. Season it with pepper and salt.

Top each slice with 2 mozzarella slices. Return to the air fryer and cook for 1 minute more. Drizzle the caprese toasts with olive oil and top with chopped basil.

Nutrition:

Calories 147 Fat 14.3g

Carbs 8.1g Protein 7.9g

3.   Cinnamon-Orange Toast

Preparation 5 minutes Cooking 10 minutes Servings: 6

Ingredients:

12 slices bread ½ cup sugar 1 stick butter

1½ tbsp. vanilla extract

1½ tbsp. cinnamon

2 oranges, zested

Directions:

In a microwave-proof bowl, mix butter, sugar and vanilla extract. Warm and stir the mixture for 30 seconds until everything melts. Add in orange zest.

Pour the mixture over bread slices. Lay the bread slices in your air fryer's cooking basket and cook for 5 minutes at 400 F. Serve with fresh banana and berry sauce.

Nutrition:

Calories 187 Fat 4g

Carbs 32g Protein 6g

4.   Herby Parmesan Bagel

Preparation Time: 5 minutes

Cooking Time: 6 minutes

Servings: 1

Ingredients:

2 tbsp. butter, softened

1 tsp. dried basil

1 tsp. dried parsley

1 tsp. garlic powder

1 tbsp. Parmesan cheese

salt and black pepper to taste

1 bagel

Directions:

Preheat the air fryer to 370 degrees. Cut the bagel in half. Place in the air fryer and cook for 3 minutes. Combine the butter, Parmesan, garlic, basil, and parsley in a small bowl. Season it with pepper and salt, to taste. Spread the mixture onto the toasted bagel. Return the bagel to the air fryer and cook for an additional 3 minutes.

Nutrition:

Calories 330

Fat 9g

Carbs 46g

Protein 19.5g

5.   Porridge with Honey & Peanut Butter

Preparation Time: 5 minutes Cooking Time: 5 minutes

Servings: 4

Ingredients:

2 cups steel-cut oats 1 cup flax seeds 1 tbsp. peanut butter

1 tbsp. butter

4 cups milk

4 tbsp. honey

Directions:

Preheat the air fryer to 390 F. Combine all of the ingredients in an ovenproof bowl. Place in the air fryer and cook for 5 minutes. Stir and serve.

Nutrition:

Calories 218.6

Fat 14.9g

Carbs 17.4g

Protein 0.3g

6.   Classic Bacon & Egg English Muffin

Preparation Time: 5 minutes Cooking Time: 7 minutes

Servings: 1

Ingredients:

1 egg 1 English muffin 2 slices of bacon

Salt and black pepper to taste

Directions:

Preheat the air fryer to 395 F. Crack the egg into a ramekin.
Place the muffin, egg and bacon in the air fryer. Cook for 6
minutes. Let cool slightly so you can assemble the sandwich.
Cut the muffin in half. Place the egg on one half and season
it with pepper and salt. Arrange the bacon on top. Top with
the other muffin half.

Nutrition:

Calories 174.3 Fat 3.9g Carbs 8.4g Protein 13.3g

7.   Peppery Sausage & Parsley Patties

Preparation Time: 6 minutes

Cooking Time: 15 minutes Servings: 4

Ingredients:

1 lb. ground Italian sausage

¼ cup breadcrumbs

1 tsp. dried parsley

1 tsp. red pepper flakes

½ tsp. salt

¼ tsp. black pepper

¼ tsp. garlic powder

1 egg beaten

Directions:

Preheat the air fryer to 350 F. Combine all of the ingredients in a large bowl. Line a baking sheet with parchment paper. Make patties out of the sausage mixture and arrange them on the baking sheet.

Cook for 15 minutes, flipping once halfway through cooking.

Nutrition:

Calories 301

Fat 27g

Carbs 2g

Protein 12g

8.   Madagascan Stew

Preparation 5 minutes Cooking: 19 minutes Servings: 4

Ingredients:

7 oz. baby new potatoes

1 tbsp. oil ½ onion, finely diced

1 ¼ cups canned black beans, drained

1 ¼ cups canned kidney beans, drained

3 cloves garlic, minced

1 tbsp. pureed ginger 2 large tomatoes, chopped

1 tbsp. tomato puree

Salt

Black pepper 1 cup vegetable stock

½ tbsp. cornstarch 1 tbsp. water

1 large handful arugula Cooked rice, to serve (optional)

Directions:

Cut the potatoes into quarters and toss them with cooking oil.

Place the potatoes in the air fryer basket.

Add onion to the basket and continue air frying for another 4 minutes.

Transfer them to a saucepan and place over medium heat.

Add garlic, ginger, beans, tomatoes, seasoning, vegetable stock, and tomato puree.

Mix cornstarch with water in a bowl and pour into the pan.

Simmer this mixture for 15 minutes.

Add arugula and cook for another 4 minutes.

Serve with rice.

Nutrition:

Calories 398 Total Fat 13.8 g

Saturated Fat 5.1 g Cholesterol 200 mg

Sodium 272 mg

Total Carbs 53.6 g

Fiber 1 g

Sugar 1.3 g

Protein 11.8 g

9.   Bacon Cheddar Chicken Fingers

Preparation Time: 10 minutes

Cooking Time: 20 minutes

Servings: 4

Ingredients:

For the chicken fingers:

1 lb. chicken tenders, about 8 pieces

Cooking spray (canola oil)

Cheddar cheese - 1 cup, shredded

Two eggs, large

1/3 cup bacon bits

2 tbsp. water

For the breading:

1 tsp. of onion powder

Panko breadcrumbs - 2 cups

Black pepper - 1 tsp., freshly ground

Paprika - 2 tbsp.

Garlic powder - 1 tsp.

Salt - 2 tsp.

Directions:

Set the air fryer to the temperature of 360°F.

In a glass dish, whip the water and eggs until combined. Use a zip lock bag, shake the garlic powder, salt, breadcrumbs, cayenne, onion powder, and pepper together. Immerse the chicken into the eggs and shake in the Ziploc bag until fully covered. Dip again in the egg mixture and back into the seasonings until a thick coating is present. Remove the tenders from the bag and set in the frying pan in the basket. Do them in batches if need to not over pack the pan. Apply the canola oil spray to the top of the tenders and heat for 6 minutes. Flip the tenders to the other side. Steam for another 4 minutes. Blend the bacon bits and shredded cheese in a dish. Evenly dust the bacon and cheese onto the hot tenders and fry for 2 more minutes.

Remove and serve while hot.

Nutrition:

Calories: 341 Fat: 11g Cholesterol: 31.5g Fiber: 1g Protein:

28g

10. Banana Oats

Preparation Time: 5 minutes

Cooking Time: 20 minutes

Servings: 2

Ingredients:

1 cup old fashioned oats

½ teaspoon baking powder

2 tablespoons sugar

½ teaspoon vanilla extract

1 banana, peeled and mashed

½ cup milk

½ cup heavy cream 1 egg, whisked

1 tablespoon butter Cooking spray

Directions:

In a bowl, mix the oats with the baking powder, sugar, and other ingredients except for the cooking spray and whisk well. Divide the mixture into 2 ramekins.

Grease the air fryer with cooking spray and preheat at 340F.

Place the ramekins in the air fryer and cook for 20 minutes.

Serve.

Nutrition:

Calories: 533

Fat: 25.8g

Carb: 57.9g

Protein: 11.5g

CHAPTER 2

Mains

11.   Mustard Lamb Loin Chops

Preparation Time: 15 minutes

Cooking Time: 30 minutes

Servings: 4

Ingredients:

4-ounces lamb loin chops

2 tablespoons Dijon mustard

1 tablespoon fresh lemon juice

½ teaspoon olive oil

1 teaspoon dried tarragon

Salt and black pepper, to taste

Directions:

Preheat the Air fryer to 390 o F and grease an Air fryer basket. Mix the mustard, lemon juice, oil, tarragon, salt, and black pepper in a large bowl. Coat the chops generously with the mustard mixture and arrange in the Air fryer basket. Cook for about 15 minutes, flipping once in between and dish out to serve hot.

Nutrition:

Calories 433 Fat 17.6g Carbohydrates 0.6g

Protein 64.1g

12.   Pesto Coated Rack of Lamb

Preparation Time: 15 minutes

Cooking Time: 15 minutes

Servings: 4

Ingredients:

½ bunch fresh mint

1½-pounds rack of lamb

1 garlic clove

¼ cup extra-virgin olive oil

½ tablespoon honey

Salt and black pepper, to taste

Directions:

Preheat the Air fryer to 200 o F and grease an Air fryer basket.

Put the mint, garlic, oil, honey, salt, and black pepper in a

blender and pulse until smooth to make pesto. Coat the rack

of lamb with this pesto on both sides and arrange in the Air fryer basket. Cook for about 15 minutes and cut the rack into individual chops to serve.

Nutrition:

Calories 406 Fat 27.7g Carbohydrates 2.9g Protein 34.9g

13.   Spiced Lamb Steaks

Preparation Time: 15 minutes

Cooking Time: 15 minutes

Servings: 3

Ingredients:

½ onion, roughly chopped

1½ pounds boneless lamb sirloin steaks

5 garlic cloves, peeled

1 tablespoon fresh ginger, peeled

1 teaspoon garam masala

1 teaspoon ground fennel

½ teaspoon ground cumin

½ teaspoon ground cinnamon

½ teaspoon cayenne pepperSalt and black pepper, to taste

Directions:

Preheat the Air fryer to 330 o F and grease an Air fryer basket.

Put the onion, garlic, ginger, and spices in a blender and pulse until smooth. Coat the lamb steaks with this mixture on both sides and refrigerate to marinate for about 24 hours.

Arrange the lamb steaks in the Air fryer basket and cook for about 15 minutes, flipping once in between. Dish out the steaks on a platter and serve warm.

Nutrition:

Calories 252 Fat 16.7g Carbohydrates 4.2g Protein 21.7g

14. Leg of Lamb with Brussels Sprout

Preparation Time: 20 minutes

Cooking Time: 1 hour 30 minutes

Servings: 6

Ingredients:

2¼ pounds leg of lamb

1 tablespoon fresh rosemary, minced

1 tablespoon fresh lemon thyme

1½ pounds Brussels sprouts, trimmed

3 tablespoons olive oil, divided

1 garlic clove, minced

Salt and ground black pepper, as required

2 tablespoons honey

Directions:

Preheat the Air fryer to 300 o F and grease an Air fryer basket.

Make slits in the leg of lamb with a sharp knife. Mix 2

tablespoons of oil, herbs, garlic, salt, and black pepper in a bowl.

Cook for about 75 minutes and set the Air fryer to 390 o F. Coat the Brussels sprout evenly with the remaining oil and honey and arrange them in the Air fryer basket with a leg of lamb.

Cook for about 15 minutes and dish out to serve warm.

Nutrition:

Calories 449

Fats 19.9g

Carbohydrates 16.6g

Proteins 51.7g

15. Honey Mustard Cheesy Meatballs

Preparation Time: 15 minutes

Cooking Time: 15 minutes

Servings: 8

Ingredients:

2 onions, chopped

1 pound ground beef

4 tablespoons fresh basil, chopped

2 tablespoons cheddar cheese, grated

2 teaspoons garlic paste

2 teaspoons honey

Salt and black pepper, to taste

2 teaspoons mustard

Directions:

Preheat the Air fryer to 385 o F and grease an Air fryer basket.

Mix all the ingredients in a bowl until well combined. Shape

the mixture into equal-sized balls gently and arrange the

meatballs in the Air fryer basket. Cook for about 15 minutes and dish out to serve warm.

Nutrition:

Calories 134

Fat 4.4g

Carbohydrates 4.6g

Sugar: 2.7g

Protein 18.2g

16.   Spicy Mexican Beef with Cotija Cheese

Preparation Time: 15 minutes

Cooking Time:15 minutes

Servings:6

Ingredients:

3 eggs, whisked

1/3 cup finely grated cotija cheese

1 cup parmesan cheese

6 minute steaks2 tablespoons Mexican spice blend

1 ½ tablespoons olive oil

Fine sea salt and ground black pepper, to taste

Directions:

Begin by sprinkling minute steaks with Mexican spice blend, salt and pepper.

Take a mixing dish and thoroughly combine the oil, cotija cheese, and parmesan cheese. In a separate mixing dish, beat the eggs.

Firstly, dip minute steaks in the egg; then, dip them in the cheese mixture.

Air-fry for 15 minutesat 345 degrees F; work in batches. Bon appétit!

Nutrition:

397 Calories

23g Fat

3.5g Carbs

41.2g Protein

0.4g Sugars

0g Fiber

CHAPTER 3

Sides

17.   Potato Fries

Preparation Time: 5 minutes

Cooking Time: 25 minutes

Servings: 4

Ingredients:

4 Medium potatoes (peeled, chopped into fries)

 4 tablespoonOlive oil

Salt and Pepper - to taste

Directions:

Toss the potatoes in oil and place in an air fryer preheated to

360 degrees Fahrenheit. Cook for around 2 minutes and then

toss it. Cook for an additional 8 minutes and then toss again. Cook for yet another 15 minutes. Serve seasoned with salt and pepper.

Nutrition:

Calories 147

Fat 23g

Protein 12.9g

18. Crispy Potato Wedges

Preparation Time: 2 minutes

Cooking Time: 25 minutes Servings: 4

Ingredients:

4 Large potatoes (peeled, chopped into wedges)

1 tablespoon Olive oil

Cajun Spice

Salt and Pepper

Directions:

Toss the potatoes in oil and place in an air fryer preheated to 375 degrees Fahrenheit. Cook for around 25 minutes, tossing thrice in between to ensure the wedges are cooked evenly. Season it with pepper and salt.

Nutrition:

Calories 154

Fat 12g

Protein 18g

19.   Curly Fries

Preparation Time: 2 minutesCooking Time: 15 minutes

Servings: 4

Ingredients:

2 Large potatoes (peeled, spiralized as curls

2 tablespoon Olive oil

 2 tablespoon Coconut oil

Salt and Pepper

1 tablespoon Tomato Ketchup

Directions:

Toss the potatoes in olive oil and coconut oil and place in an air fryer preheated to 360 degrees Fahrenheit. Cook for around 15 minutes, tossing once in between to ensure they are cooked evenly. Season it with pepper and salt. Toss in some tomato ketchup.

Nutrition:

Calories 130 Fat 10.4g Protein 6g

20. Vegetable Fries

Preparation Time: 5 minutes

Cooking Time: 15 minutes

Servings: 4

Ingredients:

5 ¼ oz. Sweet potatoes (peeled, chopped as chips)

5 ¼ oz. Courgette (peeled, chopped as chips)

 5 ¼ oz. Carrots (peeled, chopped as chips)

1 teaspoon Olive oil

Thyme

Mixed spice

Basil

Salt and Pepper

Directions:

Toss the veggies in olive oil and place in an air fryer preheated

to 360 degrees Fahrenheit.

Cook for around 18 minutes, tossing twice in between to ensure they are cooked evenly. Season with salt, pepper and the rest of the seasonings.

Nutrition:

Calories 120

Fat 9g

Protein 5.4g

21. Honey Cauliflower Bites

Preparation Time: 5 minutes

Cooking Time: 20 minutes

Servings: 4

Ingredients:

1 Cauliflower

1/3 cup Oats

1/3 cup Plain flour

1/3 cup Desiccated coconut

1 Egg (beaten)

2 tablespoon Honey

1 teaspoon Garlic puree

2 tablespoon Soy sauce

1 teaspoon Mixed spice

1 teaspoon Mixed herbs

½ teaspoon Mustard Powder

Salt and Pepper

Directions:

Preheat the air fryer to 360 degrees Fahrenheit. Combine the flour, oats and coconut in a bowl, seasoning it with salt and pepper.

Place the egg in another bowl. Season the cauliflower florets with the mixed herbs, salt and pepper. Dip the florets in egg and then dredge it with the coconut mix. Cook in the air fryer for 15 minutes. Mix together the remaining Ingredients: in a bowl.

Dip the cauliflower in the honey mixture and cook for another 5 minutes in the air fryer.

Nutrition:

Calories 160 Fat 15g Protein 12g

22. Rosemary Flavored Roast Potatoes

Preparation Time: 2 minutes

Cooking Time: 10 minutes

Servings: 4

Ingredients:

2 Potatoes

1 teaspoon Rosemary

1 tablespoon Olive oil

Salt and Pepper

Directions:

Toss the potatoes in oil and cook in an air fryer at 360 degrees Fahrenheit. Toss the roasted potatoes with salt, pepper and rosemary.

Nutrition:

Calories 165 Fat 23g Protein 8g

23. Roasted Brussels Sprouts

Preparation Time: 2 minutes

Cooking Time: 15 minutes

Servings: 4

Ingredients:

1 pound

Fresh Brussels sprouts (tough leaves discarded)

½ teaspoon kosher salt

5 teaspoons Olive oil

 Directions:

Toss the Brussels sprouts with the salt and oil. Place the sprouts in an air fryer basket at 390 degrees Fahrenheit for 15 minutes.

Nutrition:

Calories 128

Fat 10g

Protein 7g

24. Garlic Roasted Mushrooms

Preparation Time: 5 minutes

Cooking Time: 30 minutes

Servings: 4

Ingredients:

2 pound Mushrooms

1 tablespoon Duck fat

½ teaspoon Garlic powder

2 teaspoons Herbes de Provence

2 tablespoons White vermouth

 Directions:

Place the duck fat, Herbes de Provence and garlic powder in an air fryer pan and heat for 2 minutes. Stir in the mushrooms. Cook for around 25 minutes. Mix in the vermouth and cook for an additional 5 minutes.

Nutrition:

Calories 92 Fat 3.9g Protein 0.1g

CHAPTER 4

Fish and Seafood

25.   Citrus Cilantro Catfish

Preparation Time: 5 minutes

Cooking Time: 10 minutes

Servings: 2

Ingredients:

2 catfish fillets

2 tsp blackening seasoning

Juice of 1 lime

2 tbsp butter, melted

1 garlic clove, mashed

2 tbsp fresh cilantro, chopped

Directions

In a bowl, blend garlic, lime juice, cilantro, and butter. Pour half of the mixture over the fillets and sprinkle with blackening seasoning. Place the fillets in the basket and press Start. Cook for 15 minutes at 360 F on Air fryer oven function. Serve the fish topped with the remaining sauce.

Nutrition:

Calories 185

Fat 11g

Protein 21g

Sugar 0g

26. Salmon & Caper Cakes

Preparation Time: 10 minutes

Cooking Time: 10 minutes

Servings: 4-6

Ingredients:

8 oz salmon, cooked

1 ½ oz potatoes, mashed

A handful of capers

1 tbsp fresh parsley, chopped

Zest of 1 lemon

1 ¾ oz plain flour

Directions

Carefully flake the salmon. In a bowl, mix the salmon, zest, capers, dill, and mashed potatoes.

Form small cakes from the mixture and dust them with flour; refrigerate for 60 minutes. Preheat Beeville to 350 F. Press

Start and cook the cakes for 10 minutes on Air fryer oven function. Serve chilled.

Nutrition:

Calories 351

Fat 11g

Protein 19g

Sugar 1g

27. Parsley Catfish Fillets

Preparation Time: 15 minutes

Cooking Time: 10 minutes

Servings: 4

Ingredients:

4 catfish fillets, rinsed and dried

¼ cup seasoned fish fry

1 tbsp olive oil

1 tbsp fresh parsley, chopped

Directions

Add seasoned fish fry and fillets in a large Ziploc bag; massage well to coat. Place the fillets in the Breville basket and cook for 14-16 minutes at 360 F on Air fryer oven function. Top with parsley.

Nutrition: Calories 208 Carbohydrates 8 Fat 5g Protein 17g Sugar 0.5g

28. Old Bay Shrimp

Preparation Time: 15 minutesCooking Time: 10 minutes

Servings: 12

Ingredients:

1 lb. jumbo shrimp Salt to taste

¼ tsp old bay seasoning

⅓ tsp smoked paprika

¼ tsp chili powder

1 tbsp olive oil

Directions

Preheat Breville on Air fryer oven function to 390 F. In a bowl, add the shrimp, paprika, oil, salt, old bay seasoning, and chili powder; mix well. Place the shrimp in the oven and cook for 5 minutes.

Nutrition:

Calories 267 Fat 13g Protein 6g Sugar 3g

CHAPTER 5

Poultry

29.   Roasted Duck

Preparation Time: 10 minutes

Cooking Time: 3 hours

Servings: 12

Ingredients:

6 lb. whole Pekin duck

salt

5 garlic cloves chopped

1 lemon, chopped

Glaze

1/2 cup balsamic vinegar

1 lemon, juiced

1/4 cup honey

Directions:

Place the Pekin duck in a baking tray and add garlic, lemon, and salt on top. Whisk honey, vinegar, and honey in a bowl. Brush this glaze over the duck liberally.

Marinate overnight in the refrigerator. Remove the duck from the marinade and fix it on the rotisserie rod in the Air fryer oven. Turn the dial to select the "Air Roast" mode.

Hit the Time button and again use the dial to set the cooking time to 3 hours. Now push the Temp button and rotate the dial to set the temperature at 350 degrees F. Close its lid and allow the duck to roast. Serve warm.

Nutrition:

Calories 387 Total Fat 6 g Total Carbs 37.4 g

Fiber 2.9 g Protein 14.6 g

30. Honey Cajun Chicken Thigh

Preparation Time: 35 minutes Cooking Time: 30 minutes

Servings: 6

Ingredients:

1/2 cup buttermilk

1 tsp. hot sauce

1/4 cup all-purpose flour

4 tsp. honey

1/3 cup tapioca flour

1/2 tsp. garlic salt

2 1/2 tsp. Cajun seasoning

1/2 tsp. honey powder

1/4 tsp. ground paprika 1/8 tsp. cayenne pepper

1 1/2 pounds skinless, boneless chicken thighs

Directions:

Mix buttermilk and hot sauce in a re-sealable plastic bag. Put chicken thighs and marinate for 30 minutes

Mix flour, tapioca flour, Cajun seasoning, garlic salt, honey powder, paprika, and cayenne pepper in a bowl. Take it out the thighs from buttermilk mixture and dredge through flour mixture.

Remove excess flour. Preheat an air fryer toaster oven to 360 degrees F (175 degrees C). Put chicken thighs into the air fryer basket and cook for about 25 minutes.

An instant read thermometer should be inserted into the center and should read at least 165 degrees F (74 degrees C). Take out chicken thighs from air fryer and drizzle with 1 tsp. honey.

Nutrition:

Calories: 248

Fat: 12g Protein: 19g

Carbs: 16g

Fiber: 1g

31.   Taco Wrapped Chicken Thigh

Preparation Time: 60 minutes

Cooking Time: 30 minutes

Servings: 4

Ingredients:

1/2 stick butter

2 tsp. minced garlic

1/4 tsp. dried thyme

1/4 tsp. dried basil

4 Tacos

1/8 tsp. coarse salt

Freshly ground black pepper

1 1/2 lb. boneless skinless chicken thighs

Directions:

Mix softened butter, garlic, thyme, basil, salt, and pepper in a

bowl. Add butter on a piece of wax paper and roll up rightly

to form a butter log.

Refrigerate it until firm, about 2 hours. Lay one taco flat on a piece of wax paper. Place chicken thigh on top of the taco and sprinkle with garlic. Now open up the chicken thigh.

Put 2 tsp of the cold finishing butter in the middle of the chicken thigh. Tuck one end of Taco into the middle of the chicken thigh. Fold over the chicken thigh and roll the taco around the chicken thigh. Do same with remaining thighs and tacos.

Preheat an air fryer toaster oven to 370 degrees F (190 degrees C). Put chicken thighs in the basket of the air fryer oven and cook until chicken is no longer pink, and the juices run clear, about 25 minutes. An instant read thermometer should be inserted near the bone so that it should read 165 degrees F (74 degrees C).

Nutrition:

Calories: 513 Fat: 33g Protein: 32g Carbs: 15g

Fiber: 3g

CHAPTER 6

Meat

32. Paprika Pork Kabobs

Preparation Time: 10minutes

Cooking Time: 20 minutes

Servings: 4

Ingredients:

1 lb. pork tenderloin, cubed

salt and black pepper to taste

1 green bell pepper, cut into chunks

1 red onion, sliced

1 tbsp. oregano

1 tsp. smoked paprika

1 zucchini, cut into chunks

Directions:

Preheat the air fryer to 350 F. Spray the air fryer basket with cooking spray. In a bowl, mix the pork, paprika, salt, and black pepper. Thread the vegetables and pork cubes alternately onto small bamboo skewers. Spray with cooking spray and transfer to the frying basket. Bake for 15 minutes, flipping once halfway through. Serve sprinkled with oregano.

Nutrition:

Calories 342.5

Fat 13g

Protein 0g

33. Pork, Red Pepper & Mushroom Pinchos

Preparation Time: 10 minutesCooking Time: 20 minutes

Servings: 4

Ingredients:

1 lb. pork tenderloin, cubed

2 tbsp. olive oil

1 lime, juiced and zested

2 cloves garlic, minced

1 tsp. chili powder

1 tsp. ground fennel seeds

1 tsp. ground cumin

salt and white pepper to taste

1 red pepper, cut into chunks

½ cup mushrooms, quartered

Directions:

In a bowl, mix half of the olive oil, lime zest and juice, garlic, chili, ground fennel, cumin, salt, and white pepper. Add in the pork and stir to coat. Cover with cling film and place in the fridge for 1 hour. Preheat the air fryer to 380 F. Spray the air fryer basket with cooking spray. Season the mushrooms and red pepper with salt and pepper and drizzle with the remaining olive oil. Remove the pork from the fridge. Thread alternate the pork, mushroom, and red pepper pieces onto short skewers. Place in the fryer's basket. Air Fry for 15 minutes, turning once. Serve warm.

Nutrition:

Calories 714

Fat 72g

Protein 51g

34. Bacon-Wrapped & Stuffed Pork Tenderloin

Preparation Time: 10 minutes

Cooking Time: 40 minutes

Servings: 4

Ingredients:

16 bacon slices

1 lb. pork tenderloin, butterflied

salt and black pepper to taste

1 cup spinach

3 oz. cream cheese

1 small onion, sliced

1 tbsp. olive oil

1 clove garlic, minced

½ tsp. dried thyme ½ tsp. dried rosemary

Directions:

Place the tenderloin on a chopping board, cover it with a plastic wrap and pound it using a kitchen hammer to a 2-

inches flat and square piece. Trim the uneven sides with a knife to have a perfect square; remove to a plate. On the same chopping board, place and weave the bacon slices into a square the size of the pork. Place the pork on the bacon weave, and set aside.

Heat olive oil in a skillet over medium heat and sauté onion and garlic until transparent, about 3 minutes. Add in spinach, rosemary, thyme, salt, and pepper and cook until the spinach wilts. Stir in cream cheese, until the mixture is even. Turn the heat off.

Preheat the air fryer to 360 F. Spread the spinach mixture onto the pork loin. Roll up bacon and pork over the spinach stuffing. Secure the ends with toothpicks. Place in the fryer's basket and Bake for 15 minutes. Turn them and cook for 5 more minutes until golden. Let sit for 4 minutes before slicing.

Nutrition: Calories 742 Fat 52.6g Protein 18g

35. Hungarian-Style Pork Chops

Preparation Time: 5 minutes

Cooking Time: 15 minutes

Servings: 4

Ingredients:

1 lb. pork chops, boneless

2 tbsp. olive oil

2 tsp. Hungarian paprika

1 ground bay leaf

½ tsp. dried thyme

1 tsp. garlic powder

salt and black pepper to taste

¼ cup yogurt

2 garlic cloves, minced

Directions:

Preheat the air fryer to 380 F. Spray the air fryer basket with

cooking spray. Mix the Hungarian paprika, ground bay leaf,

thyme, garlic powder, salt, and black pepper in a bowl. Rub the pork with the mixture, drizzle with some olive oil and place them in the fryer's basket. Air Fry for 15 minutes, turning once. Mix yogurt with garlic, the remaining oil, and salt. Serve with the chops.

Nutrition:

Calories 462

Fat 29g

Protein 17g

36.   Pork Lettuce Cups

Preparation Time: 10 minutes

Cooking Time: 25 minutes

Servings: 4

Ingredients:

1 tbsp. sesame oil

1lb. pork tenderloin, sliced

½ white onion, sliced

2 tbsp. sesame seeds, toasted

2 Little Gem lettuces, leaves separated

1 cup radishes cut into matchsticks

1 tsp. red chili flakes 2 tbsp. teriyaki sauce

1 tsp. honey salt and black pepper to taste

Directions:

In a bowl, combine teriyaki sauce, red chili flakes, honey, sesame oil, salt, and pepper. Add in the pork, toss to coat, and place in the fridge covered for 30 minutes.

Preheat the air fryer to 360 F. Grease the air fryer basket with cooking spray. Remove the pork from the marinade and place it in the frying basket, reserving the marinate liquid. Air Fry for 12 minutes, flipping once. Arrange the lettuce leaves on a serving platter and divide the pork between them. Top with onion, radishes, and sesame seeds. Drizzle with the reserved marinade and serve.

Nutrition:

Calories 884

Fat 52g

Protein 18.3g

CHAPTER 7

Vegetables

37. Feta & Mushroom Frittata

Preparation Time: 10 minutes

Cooking Time: 30 minutes

Servings: 4

Ingredients:

1 red onion, thinly sliced

4 cups button mushrooms, thinly sliced

salt to taste

6 tbsp. feta cheese, crumbled

6 medium eggs

non-stick cooking spray

2 tbsp. olive oil

Directions:

Sauté the onion and mushrooms in olive oil over medium heat until the vegetables are tender. Remove the vegetables from the pan and drain on a paper towel-lined plate. In a mixing bowl, whisk eggs and salt. Coat all sides of the baking dish with cooking spray. Preheat your air fryer to 325°Fahrenheit. Pour the beaten eggs into a baking dish and scatter the sautéed vegetables and crumble feta on top. Bake in the air fryer for 30-minutes. Allow to cool slightly and serve!

Nutrition:

Calories 226

Fat 9.3g

Carbs 8.7g

Protein 12.6g

38. Vegetarian Hash Browns

Preparation Time: 10 minutes

Cooking Time: 19 minutes

Servings: 8

Ingredients:

4 large potatoes, peeled, shredded

1 tsp. onion powder

1 tsp. garlic powder

2 tsp. chili flakes

salt and pepper to taste

2 tsp. corn flour

2 tsp. olive oil

cooking spray as needed

Directions:

Add potatoes to a bowl of cold water and leave them to soak for a few minutes then drain them and repeat. Add a teaspoon of olive oil into the skillet and cook potatoes over medium heat for 4-minutes. Place potatoes on a plate to cool once they are cooked. In a large mixing bowl, add flour, potatoes, salt, pepper and other seasonings and combine well. Place the bowl in the fridge for 20-minutes. Preheat your air fryer to 350°Fahrenheit. Remove hash browns from the fridge and cut into size pieces you desire. Spray the wire basket of your air fryer with some oil, add the hash browns and fry them for 15-minutes. Halfway through flip them to help cook them all over. Serve hot!

Nutrition:

Calories 242

Fat 13.1g

Carbs 9.6g

Protein 14.2g

39. Tofu Frittata

Preparation Time: 20 minutes

Cooking Time: 40 minutes

Servings: 4

Ingredients:

1 flax egg (1 tbsp. flax meal + 3 tablespoons water)

1 ¾ cups brown rice, cooked

1 tbsp. olive oil

½ onion, chopped

4 spring onions, chopped

handful of basil leaves, chopped

2 tsp. arrowroot powder

2/3 cup almond milk

3 tbsp. nutritional yeast

2 tbsp. soy sauce

2 tsp. Dijon mustard

1 package firm tofu

½ cup baby spinach, chopped

½ cup kale, chopped

1 yellow pepper, chopped

3 big mushrooms, chopped

½ tsp. turmeric

4 cloves of garlic, crushed

Directions:

Preheat your air fryer to 375°Fahrenheit. Grease a pan that will fit into the air fryer the frittata crust by mixing the brown rice and flax egg. Press the rice mix onto the baking dish until the crust is formed. Brush little olive oil on rice mix and cook for 10-minutes. Meanwhile, add the remaining olive oil to the skillet and heat, then sauté the garlic and onions for 2-minutes. Add the mushrooms and pepper and continue to sauté for an additional 3-minutes. Stir in the spinach, kale, spring onions and basil. Remove from the pan and set aside. In a food processor, pulse the tofu, mustard, turmeric, nutritional yeast, soy sauce, almond milk and arrowroot powder. Pour into a mixing bowl and stir in the sautéed vegetables. Pour veggie mix over the rice crust and cook in an air fryer for 40-minutes. Serve warm.

Nutrition:

Calories 132

Fat 10.2g

Carbs 0.6g

Protein 3.2g

40.   Onion Pakora

Preparation Time: 5 minutes

Cooking Time: 6 minutes

Servings: 6

Ingredients:

 1 cup graham flour

¼ tsp. turmeric powder

salt to taste

1/8 tsp. chili powder

¼ tsp. carom

1 tbsp. fresh coriander, chopped

2 green chili peppers, finely chopped

4 onions, finely chopped

2 tsp. vegetable oil ¼ cup rice flour

Directions:

Combine the flours and oil in a mixing bowl. Add water as needed to create a dough-like consistency. Add peppers, onions, coriander, carom, chili powder, and turmeric. Preheat the air fryer to 350°Fahrenheit. Roll vegetable mixture into small balls, add to the fryer and cook for about 6-minutes. Serve with hot sauce!

Nutrition:

Calories 253

Fat 12.2g

Carbs 11.4g

Protein 7.6g

CHAPTER 8

Soup and Stews

41.   Low Carb Taco Soup

Preparation Time: 25 minutes

Cooking Time: 20 minutes

Servings: 4

Ingredients:

1 tbsp. olive oil

2 lbs. ground beef

1 onion, diced

1 bell pepper, diced

2 tbsp. garlic, minced

2 tbsp. cumin

1 tsp. paprika

1 tsp. salt

1 tsp. pepper

1 cup shredded cheese

1 tsp. Sriracha

14.5 oz. can tomato, diced

4 oz. can green chilies

2 cups beef broth

2 tbsp. chili powder

Directions:

In a pan that fits the air fryer oven, mix all the ingredients, toss, introduce in the fryer and cook at 380°F for 20 minutes

Divide the stew into bowls and serve for lunch.

Nutrition:

Calories 183 Fat 4g Fiber 2g Carbohydrates 4g

Protein 12g

CHAPTER 9

Snacks

42. Crispy Eggplant

Preparation Time: 5 minutes

Cooking Time: 20 minutes Servings: 4

Ingredients:

1 eggplant, cut into 1-inch pieces

1/2 tsp Italian seasoning

1 tsp paprika

1/2 tsp red pepper

1 tsp garlic powder 2 tbsp olive oil

Directions:

Add all ingredients into the large mixing bowl and toss well.

Transfer eggplant mixture into the air fryer oven basket.

Cook at 375 F for 20 minutes. Shake basket halfway through.

Serve and enjoy.

Nutrition:

Calories 99 Fat 7.5 g Carbohydrates 8.7 g

Sugar 4.5 g Protein 1.5 g Cholesterol 0 mg

43. Steak Nuggets

Preparation Time: 10 minutes

Cooking Time: 15 minutes

Servings: 4

Ingredients:

1 lb. beef steak, cut into chunks

1 large egg, lightly beaten

1/2 cup pork rind, crushed

1/2 cup parmesan cheese, grated

1/2 tsp salt

Directions:

Add egg in a small bowl.

In a shallow bowl, mix together pork rind, cheese, and salt.

Dip each steak chunk in egg then coat with pork rind mixture and place on a plate. Place in refrigerator for 30 minutes.

Spray air fryer oven basket with cooking spray.

Preheat the air fryer oven to 400 F.

Place steak nuggets in air fryer oven basket and cook for 15-18 minutes or until cooked. Shake after every 4 minutes.

Serve and enjoy.

Nutrition:

Calories 609

Fat 38 g

Carbohydrates 2 g

Sugar 0.4 g

Protein 63 g

Cholesterol 195 mg

CHAPTER 10

Desserts

44. Dried Raspberries

Preparation Time: 10 minutes

Cooking Time: 15 hours

Servings: 4

Ingredients:

4 cups raspberries, wash and dry

1/4 cup fresh lemon juice

Directions:

Add raspberries and lemon juice in a bowl and toss well.

Arrange raspberries on instant vortex air fryer oven tray and

dehydrate at 135 F for 12-15 hours.

Store in an air-tight container.

Nutrition:

Calories – 68

Protein – 1.6 g.

Fat – 0.9 g.

Carbs – 15 g.

45.　Sweet Peach Wedges

Preparation Time: 10 minutes

Cooking Time: 8 hours

Servings: 4

Ingredients:

3 peaches, cut and remove pits and sliced

1/2 cup fresh lemon juice

Directions:

Add lemon juice and peach slices into the bowl and toss well.

Arrange peach slices on instant vortex air fryer oven rack and dehydrate at 135 F for 6-8 hours.

Serve and enjoy.

Nutrition:

Calories 52

Protein –1.3 g.

Fat 0.5 g.

Carbs – 11.1 g.

46.   Air Fryer Oreo Cookies

Preparation Time: 5 minutes

Cooking Time: 5 minutes

Servings: 9

Ingredients:

Pancake Mix: ½ cup

Water: ½ cup

Cooking spray

Chocolate sandwich cookies: 9 (e.g. Oreo)

Confectioners' sugar: 1 tablespoon, or to taste

Directions:

Blend the pancake mixture with the water until well mixed.

Line the parchment paper on the basket of an air fryer. Spray

nonstick cooking spray on parchment paper. Dip each cookie

into the mixture of the pancake and place it in the basket.

Make sure they do not touch; if possible, cook in batches.

The air fryer is preheated to 400 degrees F (200 degrees C). Add basket and cook for 4 to 5 minutes; flip until golden brown, 2 to 3 more minutes. Sprinkle the sugar over the cookies and serve.

Nutrition:

Calories – 77

Protein – 1.2 g.

Fat – 2.1 g.

Carbs – 13.7 g.

47. Air Fried Butter Cake

Preparation Time: 10 minutes

Cooking Time: 15 minutes

Servings: 4

Ingredients:

7 Tablespoons of butter, at ambient temperature

White sugar: ¼ cup plus 2 tablespoons

All-purpose flour: 1 ⅔ cups

Salt: 1 pinch or to taste

Milk: 6 tablespoons

Directions:

Preheat an air fryer to 350 F (180 C). Spray the cooking spray on a tiny fluted tube pan.

Take a large bowl and add ¼ cup butter and 2 tablespoons of sugar in it.

Take an electric mixer to beat the sugar and butter until smooth and fluffy. Stir in salt and flour. Stir in the milk and thoroughly combine batter. Move batter to the prepared saucepan; use a spoon back to level the surface.

Place the pan inside the basket of the air fryer. Set the timer within 15 minutes. Bake the batter until a toothpick comes out clean when inserted into the cake.

Turn the cake out of the saucepan and allow it to cool for about five minutes.

Nutrition:

Calories – 470

Protein – 7.9 g.

Fat – 22.4 g.

Carbs – 59.7 g.

48.   Air Fryer S'mores

Preparation Time: 5 minutes

Cooking Time: 3 minutes

Servings: 4

Ingredients:

Four graham crackers (each half split to make 2 squares, for a total of 8 squares)

8 Squares of Hershey's chocolate bar, broken into squares

4 Marshmallows

Directions:

Take deliberate steps. Air-fryers use hot air for cooking food. Marshmallows are light and fluffy, and this should keep the marshmallows from flying around the basket if you follow these steps.

Put 4 squares of graham crackers on a basket of the air fryer.

Place 2 squares of chocolate bars on each cracker.

Place back the basket in the air fryer and fry on air at 390 °F for 1 minute. It is barely long enough for the chocolate to melt. Remove basket from air fryer. Top with a marshmallow over each cracker. Throw the marshmallow down a little bit into the melted chocolate. This will help to make the marshmallow stay over the chocolate.

Put back the basket in the air fryer and fry at 390 °F for 2 minutes. (The marshmallows should be puffed up and browned at the tops.)

Using tongs to carefully remove each cracker from the basket of the air fryer and place it on a platter. Top each marshmallow with another square of graham crackers.

Enjoy it right away!

Nutrition:

Calories 200 Protein 2.6 g.Fat 3.1 g.

Carbs 15.7 g.

49.   Peanut Butter Cookies

Preparation Time: 2 minutes

Cooking Time: 5 minutes

Servings: 10

Ingredients:

Peanut Butter: 1 cup

Sugar: 1 cup

1 Egg

Directions:

Blend all of the ingredients with a hand mixer.

Spray trays of air fryer with canola oil. (Alternatively, parchment paper can also be used, but it will take longer to cook your cookies)

Set the air fryer temperature to 350 degrees and preheat it.

Place rounded dough balls onto air fryer trays. Press down softly with the back of a fork.

Place air fryer tray in your air fryer in the middle place. Cook for five minutes.

Use milk to serve with cookies.

Nutrition:

Calories 236

Protein 6 g.

Fat 13 g.

Carbs 26 g.

50.   Sweet Pear Stew

Preparation Time: 10 minutes

Cooking Time: 15 minutes

Servings: 4

Ingredients:

4 pears, cored and cut into wedges

1 tsp vanilla

1/4 cup apple juice

2 cups grapes, halved

Directions:

Put all of the ingredients in the inner pot of air fryer and stir well. Seal pot and cook on high for 15 minutes.

As soon as the cooking is done, let it release pressure naturally for 10 minutes then release remaining using quick release. Remove lid.

Nutrition: Calories 162 Protein 1.1 g. Fat 0.5 g. Carbs – 41.6 g.

Conclusion

U nlike frying things in a typical pan on gas which fails to make your fries crisp and leaves your samosa uncooked due to uneven heat. The inbuilt kitchen deep fryers do it all; you can have perfectly crisp French fries like the one you get in restaurants. Your samosas will be perfectly cooked inside- out. Well, the list doesn't end here it goes on and on the potato wedges, chicken and much more. You can make many starters and dishes using fryer and relish the taste buds of your loved ones.

The new air fryers come along with a lot of features, so you don't mess up doing things enjoy your cooking experience. The free hot to set the temperature according to your convenience both mechanically and electronically. Oil filters to reuse the oil and use it for a long run. With the ventilation system to reduce and eliminate the frying odor. In a few models you also get the automatic timers and alarm set for convenient cooking, frying I mean. Also, the auto- push and raise feature to immerse or hold back the frying basket to achieve the perfect frying aim. So, why should you wait? I am sure you don't want to mess in your kitchen when grilling, baking of frying your food, right? Get yourself an air fryer. Thank you for purchasing this cookbook I hope you will apply all the acquired knowledge productively.

CPSIA information can be obtained
at www.ICGtesting.com
Printed in the USA
BVHW092055040621
608822BV00004B/1039